Copyright © 2025 by Holly Symons
All rights reserved.

No part of this book may be reproduced, scanned, or distributed in any printed or electronic form without permission. This book is a work of fiction. Names, characters, places, and incidents are either the product of the author's imagination or used fictitiously.
Hardback - ISBN: 978-1-923567-63-4
Paperback - ISBN: 978-1-923567-64-1
eBook - ISBN: 978-1-923567-65-8

Cover design by **Holly Symons**
First Edition

For More, Please Visit

HollySymons.com.au

"This is not a lecture, it's a roast and it might just save you from dying alone with smelly socks."

No One Likes a Screaming Banshee: A Gentleman's Guide to Not Scaring Girls Away

Holly Symons

Table of Contents

Chapter One: Showers Are Not Optional   1

Daily soap + water is the bare minimum. If your armpits smell like a medieval battlefield, romance isn't in your future.

Chapter Two: Sockpocalypse Now   5

Socks that can stand up by themselves aren't "vintage", they're biohazards. Burn them, don't wear them.

Chapter Three: Dragon Breath Be Gone   9

Brushing your teeth is not optional. Chewing gum is not a substitute. Nobody wants to kiss a dragon.

Chapter Four: The Banshee Effect   12

Roaring at girls doesn't make you powerful, it makes you sound unhinged. Use words, not dinosaur calls.

Chapter Five: Hoodies, Trackies & Stains   15

Comfort is fine. Looking like you rolled in yesterday's lunch? Not fine.

Chapter Six: Rage Quitting Life   18

Punching walls and controllers doesn't make you look tough, it makes you look like you're losing to your own emotions.

Chapter Seven: The Grunt Isn't a Love Language   21

Communicating in grunts and monosyllables won't charm anyone. Words are your secret weapon.

Chapter Eight: Conversations, Not Quests   24

Girls are not NPCs waiting to hand you side missions. Speak like a human, not a gamer script.

Chapter Nine: Meme Lords Don't Get Queens   27

Your TikTok references aren't flirting. Memes don't count as personality.

Chapter Ten: Texting Is Not Morse Code   30

Sending 47 messages in a row doesn't make you romantic it makes you a stalker with Wi-Fi.

Chapter Eleven: Flexing Fails   33

No girl has ever swooned because a guy lifted a chair with one hand. Confidence beats showing off.

Chapter Twelve: Fast Food Fingers   36

Chicken nuggets are not finger jewelry. Eat like you've seen utensils before.

Chapter Thirteen: Hair Today, Gone Tomorrow   39

Gelled helmets and mullets aren't the flex you think they are. Wash, trim, repeat.

Chapter Fourteen: Manners Make the Man   42

"Please" and "thank you" aren't old-fashioned. They're the cheat codes to not being a jerk.

Chapter Fifteen: Chill, Romeo   45

Day two love poems and marriage proposals = Red Flag. Slow your roll, Shakespeare.

Chapter Sixteen: Respect the Respawn   48

Rejection isn't the end of the world. Respawn, upgrade, try again without throwing shade.

Chapter Seventeen: Smell Like a Human, Not a Locker Room 51

Deodorant: yes. Axe body spray cloud: no. Balance is everything.

Chapter Eighteen: Sports Talk Isn't Small Talk 54

Unless she's actually into it, a 15-minute breakdown of the game is not flirting it's a hostage situation.

Chapter Nineteen: The Group Chat Isn't Private 57

Anything you send will be screenshotted. Assume the entire school sees it.

Chapter Twenty: The Secret Cheat Code 60

Listening isn't boring it's literally the most attractive skill you can learn.

Chapter One: Showers Are Not Optional

Gentlemen-in-training let's get one thing straight: showers are not a luxury. They are the foundation of civilization. Forget Wi-Fi, without soap and water, society would collapse in about three days.

Take a shower. Every. Single. Day.

Not "every second day." Not "when I feel sweaty." Not "when Mum says the hallway smells like a gym sock graveyard." Every. Day.

Girls (and literally everyone else) notice hygiene before anything else. You could have the best hoodie, the smoothest playlist, and hair styled like a K-pop star, but if your scent could knock out a fruit bat at twenty paces, game over.

The Soap Struggle
Soap is not optional. Standing under water without soap is like licking a chip without salt. Pointless. Scrub with actual suds. Shampoo is also part of the deal. Your hair is not meant to double as a grease pan.

The Pit Problem
Deodorant is not a suggestion; it's a survival tool. Spray it, roll it, stick it just use it. If you skip it, your armpits become chemical warfare zones.

Pro-Tips from the Bathroom Battlefield

- The Towel Test: If your towel smells like a wet dog, congrats you're just rubbing stink back on. Wash it. Often.

- Laundry Logic: Dirty clothes go in the hamper, not in artistic piles on the floor. Your mum is not your maid.

- Bathroom Exit Strategy: Wipe down the bench, hang up your towel, and leave the bathroom looking like a human was in there not a swamp creature.

- Bonus Move: Girls notice when a guy cleans up after himself. It screams "responsible adult" instead of "feral raccoon."

Why It Matters

Nobody expects you to smell like a cologne ad, but here's the thing: if you can't manage basic hygiene, why would anyone believe you can manage a relationship?

Clean isn't about impressing someone. It's

about showing respect for yourself and for the people who have to share airspace with you.

So remember this: romance doesn't start with roses. It starts with a shower and a bathroom that doesn't look like a biohazard zone.

Chapter Two: Sockpocalypse Now

Some say the end of the world will come with fire. Others say ice. We say it will come with teenage socks, hardened, stinking relics of battles fought on bedroom floors.

Gentlemen, socks are not meant to become fossils. They are not meant to smell like toxic waste. And they are definitely not meant to be left in strange places, like under the bed, behind the couch, or in the fridge (don't laugh, it's happened).

The Sock Crime Scene
Leaving socks scattered around the house is not just gross it's a crime against anyone with a functioning nose. No girl is going to

be impressed when she sits down, looks around, and sees your sock population thriving like wild rabbits.

The Laundry Law
Here's the law: dirty socks go in the hamper. Full stop. Not in the corner. Not next to the hamper. Not "airing out" on the windowsill like a flag of surrender. In the hamper.

Mismatched Madness
Wearing mismatched socks isn't quirky. It's not a personality trait. It just makes you look like you got dressed in the dark. If one disappears into the Bermuda Triangle of washing machines, buy new ones. Socks aren't rare collector's items.

Pro-Tips from the Laundry Trenches

- The Hamper Hoop: Treat your hamper like a basketball net. Two points if you get the socks in from across the room. Zero if they're lying on the floor.
- Sock Shelf Life: If your socks have holes big enough to qualify as ventilation systems, retire them. You're not in the army you can afford fresh pairs.
- The Floor Isn't Storage: Your mum is not your sock fairy. She doesn't magically appear to pick them up.
- Bonus Move: Girls dig a guy who can do his own laundry. Trust us: knowing how to use a washing machine is hotter than flexing in front of a mirror.

Why It Matters
Socks may seem small, but they say a lot. If you can't handle looking after the tiniest

part of your wardrobe, how are you going to handle the big stuff?

So do the world a favor: conquer the Sockpocalypse before it conquers you.

Chapter Three: Dragon Breath Be Gone

So, you've showered, your socks are no longer staging a rebellion... but then you open your mouth. And bam, the smell of last night's garlic bread mixed with a hint of something that died in 2007. Congratulations, you've just ended your chances before you even said "hi."

The Basics
Brushing your teeth twice a day isn't just about dental health, it's about not clearing a room when you speak. And no, chewing gum doesn't count as brushing. Gum is a cover-up, not a cure. It's like spraying deodorant over a swamp monster.

The Tongue Trap

Here's the secret nobody tells you: bad breath doesn't just come from your teeth. It hides on your tongue. Brush it. Gently. Otherwise, you're carrying around a whole buffet of bacteria every time you talk.

Dentist = Ally, Not Enemy
Yeah, nobody likes the dentist, but skipping check-ups means you risk cavities, rotten teeth, and breath that could knock a bird out of the sky. Trust me: girls aren't impressed by "mystery smells."

Pro-Tips from the Oral Arena

- Water > Soda: Soda coats your teeth in sugar. Water rinses and refreshes. Choose wisely.
- Carry Backup: Mints or gum are fine for emergencies, but they should never replace brushing.

- Morning Check: Before you leave the house, breathe into your hand. If you recoil, imagine how others feel.
- Bonus Move: A guy with fresh breath and a smile? Instantly more attractive. It's science.

Why It Matters

Think of your mouth as your opening act. If it bombs, the whole shows cancelled. Good breath shows you care that you respect yourself, and that you're not secretly a dragon in disguise.

So remember: if you want your words to be heard, make sure they don't come with a side order of stink.

Chapter Four: The Banshee Effect

So, you see a girl you like, and your brain goes: "Quick, make a noise!" And out it comes a roar, a yell, a banshee scream that makes dogs in three suburbs start howling.

Congratulations. You didn't impress her. You terrified her.

Why It Doesn't Work
Here's the harsh truth: no girl has ever thought, "Wow, he screamed like a dying velociraptor... I must give him my number immediately."
Shouting, grunting, roaring it doesn't make you powerful, it makes you look like you were thrown at a wall as a baby and never

quite recovered.

Volume ≠ Confidence

Confidence isn't about how loud you are. It's about how you carry yourself. If you have to scream to be noticed, you're not showing confidence, you're showing desperation.

Respect the Ears
Girls have ears. Blasting them like a faulty car alarm doesn't say "romance." It says, "restraining order incoming."

Pro-Tips for the Non-Banshee Gentleman

- Inside Voices Win Hearts: Speak like you're talking to a person, not leading an army charge.

- Words > Screeches: Try "Hi, how are you?" instead of "AAAAARGHHHH!"
- The Compliment Trick: Compliments whispered at normal volume work better than shouting "NICE HAIR!" across the cafeteria.
- Bonus Move: A calm, collected guy always stands out more than the one who sounds like a blender stuck on high speed.

Why It Matters

When you yell, you don't look cool, you look unstable. When you talk like a human being, you look like someone worth knowing.

So if you want to get noticed, ditch the banshee act. Save the roaring for dinosaur movies.

Chapter Five: Hoodies, Trackies & Stains

Comfort is king, we get it. Hoodies are warm, trackies are cozy, and stains... well, stains are a lifestyle choice for some of you. But here's the thing: what you wear screams louder than you do. And if what it's screaming is "I just wrestled a pizza and lost," you've got a problem.

The Hoodie Hustle
Hoodies are fine. Hoodies are great. But a hoodie that smells like three weeks of skipped showers? Not great. A hoodie with enough crumbs to feed a family of ducks? Worse. Hoodies should say "effortlessly casual," not "I live under a bridge."

The Trackies in Trouble

Track pants = comfy. Track pants with saggy knees, rips in the wrong places, and mystery stains = tragic. If your trackies look like they survived a house fire, it's time to retire them.

Stain Nation

Food stains don't make you quirky. They don't tell the story of your life. They tell the story of your last sloppy meal. Washing machines exist. Use them.

Pro-Tips from the Wardrobe Warriors

- Rotation Rules: If you've worn it for three days straight, it's not "favorite clothes" it's a biohazard.
- Stain Control: Napkin > sleeve. Always.
- Laundry Cycle: Clothes belong in the

wash, not balled up in your bed or fermenting on the floor.

- Bonus Move: A clean, simple t-shirt beats a designer hoodie covered in spaghetti sauce every single time.

Why It Matters

First impressions stick. If you look like you don't care about your clothes, people assume you don't care about anything. You don't have to dress fancy, but you do have to dress like you've met soap and water sometime this decade.

So gentlemen, remember wear hoodies, rock trackies, live in comfort. Just don't look like you've been rescued from a dumpster.

Chapter Six: Rage Quitting Life

So, you lost a game. Or someone looked at you funny. Or your crush left you on read. And what do you do? Smash a controller, punch a wall, kick a bin like you're auditioning for WWE.

Congratulation, you didn't look tough. You looked like a toddler who just had his juice box taken away.

The Myth of the Angry Guy
Some boys think anger = strength. Spoiler: it doesn't. Anger just shows you can't handle your emotions. Anyone can throw a tantrum. Real strength is keeping calm when life throws you a curveball.

Property Damage ≠ Power

Here's the thing: that wall you just punched? It didn't flinch. That controller you snapped in half. It didn't care. All you did was make yourself look unhinged and give your mum extra repair bills.

Girls Notice and Not in a Good Way

Newsflash: no girl has ever thought, "Wow, look at the way he smashed that Xbox controller. I bet he'd be great in a relationship." Rage doesn't impress. It alarms.

Pro-Tips for Anger Management Lite

- Pause Button: When you feel the rage boiling, pause. Walk away. Deep breath. Don't Hulk out.

- Fist vs Pillow: If you must punch something, try a pillow not a wall. Walls don't heal. Your knuckles don't either.
- Cool Down Routine: Music, sports, writing anything beats looking like a volcano about to erupt.
- Bonus Move: Self-control is the real flex. A guy who can stay calm under pressure? That's rare, and it stands out.

Why It Matters

Rage quitting life doesn't just make you look unstable it makes you untrustworthy. Nobody wants to walk on eggshells around someone who explodes over small stuff.

So gentlemen, if you want to be respected, ditch the tantrums. Handle frustration like a pro, not like a banshee with a broken controller.

Chapter Seven: The Grunt Isn't a Love Language

Picture this: a girl asks you how your day was, and your response is… "Uhh." She tries again: "What's your favorite movie?" And you say… "Meh." Congratulations, you've just convinced her your part caveman.

Grunts are fine if you've stubbed your toe or just got tackled in rugby. But if they're your main form of communication, you're not mysterious you're exhausting.

The Myth of the Strong, Silent Type
Yes, movies make the brooding, quiet guy look cool. Reality check: in real life, "brooding" just feels like babysitting someone who won't talk. If she has to drag

every word out of you like pulling teeth, she'll stop trying.

Why Words Matter

Words are how you show your personality. They're how you connect. They're how you make someone laugh. Grunting isn't communication it's background noise.

Pro-Tips for Upgrading from Caveman to Gentleman

- Use Real Words: "Good," "bad," "awesome," "boring." Pick one. It's better than "uhh."
- Ask Back: If she asks how your day was, ask about hers. That's called a conversation.
- Expand a Little: You don't need an essay. One extra sentence is enough.

- Bonus Move: Humor is attractive. Words give you the power to be funny. Grunts don't.

Why It Matters
If you can't talk, she can't get to know you. And if she can't get to know you, she's not sticking around. Simple as that.

So gentlemen, retire the grunts. Upgrade to words. They're free, they're powerful, and trust me they work way better than "meh."

Chapter Eight: Conversations, Not Quests

Here's the thing: girls are not side quests. You don't walk up, grunt "Oi," and expect them to hand you a mission and a reward. They're people, not NPCs from Skyrim.

Dialogue, Not Checklists
Asking "Wanna hang out?" isn't a conversation. That's a quest prompt. Real conversations go back and forth like tennis, not like reading dialogue options off a controller screen.

Stop Farming for Answers
If you rapid-fire questions without actually listening, you're not talking, you're

interrogating. She's not a treasure chest waiting for you to unlock secrets with the right combo.

Listen for Real

Here's the power move: listen to her answers and respond like a human being. If she says she likes drawing, don't grunt "cool" and switch back to FIFA talk. Ask about it. Show interest.

Pro-Tips for Social XP Gains

- Openers Matter: "Hey, how's your day?" works way better than "sup."
- Play the Long Game: You don't win with one conversation. Relationships are built over time.
- Don't Spam: If she doesn't reply instantly, don't send 14 more "?" messages. Chill.
- Bonus Move: Remember details. If she

mentioned loving pizza, bring it up later. That's how you score XP in real life.

Why It Matters

Treating conversations like quests makes you look like you don't care who she is you just want the reward. And guess what? That's the fastest way to fail the mission.

So gentlemen, remember relationships aren't quests. They're co-op campaigns.

Chapter Nine: Meme Lords Don't Get Queens

So, you've got a meme folder bigger than your homework folder. You can quote every TikTok sound by heart. And you think sending "funny" reels at 3 a.m. is the fastest way to her heart.

Spoiler: it's not.

Memes Aren't Personality
Sharing memes is fun. Living your entire life as a meme factory? Not so much. If every reply you give is a SpongeBob gif, she's not dating you she's dating Nickelodeon.

Funny ≠ Original
Here's the thing: memes are other

people's jokes. If you only recycle them, you're not funny, you're just a walking repost account. Girls want to see you, your thoughts, your humor, your stories. Not just the "haha" you screenshotted.

DMs Aren't Stand-Up Comedy

Sliding into someone's DMs with a meme can work once in a while. But if that's your only move? You've just downgraded yourself from "potential boyfriend" to "free entertainment service."

Pro-Tips for Meme Enthusiasts

- Use Memes as Spice, Not the Meal: They're seasoning, not the whole dish.
- Mix In Your Own Jokes: Show your actual personality, not just you're For You Page.
- Read the Room: Not every meme fits

every moment. Timing is everything.

- Bonus Move: If you can make her laugh with your own wit, you've leveled up past Meme Lord into Gentleman Comedian.

Why It Matters

Memes are fun, but they don't build connections. If all you bring to the table is reposted content, you'll be remembered as "that guy who only sends TikTok's." And trust me, that's not the crown you want.

So gentlemen, enjoy your memes. Just don't confuse them for a personality. Queens want a king, not a meme dealer.

Chapter Ten: Texting Is Not Morse Code

Texting is supposed to be simple. It's words on a screen. Yet somehow, some of you treat it like you're tapping out SOS signals from a sinking ship.

The Triple Question Mark Problem
If she doesn't reply instantly, sending "???" five more times doesn't speed things up. It just makes you look like you're fighting with your own patience. Spoiler: she saw your text. She's just busy.

"WYD" Isn't Poetry
One-word texts like "wyd," "sup," or "k" are the equivalent of handing someone a blank piece of paper and expecting them to write a novel. Put in some effort.

Don't Be a Notification Nuke

Blowing up someone's phone with 37 missed texts doesn't say "romantic." It says, "restraining order." Less is more.

Pro-Tips for Texting Like a Gentleman

- Think Before You Send: If your text looks like you dropped your phone on the keyboard, rewrite it.
- Quality Beats Quantity: One thoughtful message > 20 "hey" messages.
- Respect the Pause: If she hasn't replied, let her. The world won't end.
- Bonus Move: Emojis are like hot sauce. A little adds flavor. Too much ruins the meal.

Why It Matters

Texting is your digital first impression. If you

come off clingy, lazy, or confusing, that's the picture she builds of you.

So, gentlemen, remember texting isn't Morse code. It's communication. Use your words wisely or watch her ghost you faster than your Wi-Fi cuts out during Fortnite.

Chapter Eleven: Flexing Fails

So, you've got muscles. Great. Nobody's mad about it. But here's the thing: flexing like your veins are auditioning for a Marvel movie doesn't automatically make girls swoon.

The Mirror Problem
Spending twenty minutes in the bathroom mirror flexing your arms doesn't make you look strong. It makes you look like you're on a date with yourself. Spoiler: the mirror isn't going to text you back.

Random Object Syndrome
Lifting chairs, watermelons, or your friend's little brother just to prove you're "jacked"

doesn't impress anyone. It makes people nervous that you're about to break something (or someone).

Gym Talk Overload

Yes, you can bench 200. Yes, you do "push day." Yes, protein powder is your religion. But if that's all you talk about, congratulations you're now less boyfriend material and more walking infomercial for creatine.

Pro-Tips for Strength with Style

- Flex at the Right Time: Playing sports, helping carry groceries, moving furniture practical strength beats random flexing.
- Confidence > Muscle Mass: Girls notice how you treat people more than how much you can lift.

- Chill on the Gym Stats: Nobody needs your full workout history unless they asked.
- Bonus Move: Strength mixed with humility? That's the ultimate power combo.

Why It Matters

Flexing constantly doesn't show strength, it shows insecurity. Real confidence doesn't need to announce itself every five minutes.

So gentlemen, remember: flexing isn't bad. Flexing all the time? Instant fail.

Chapter Twelve: Fast Food Fingers

Picture this: you're on a date. The food arrives. And instead of picking up a fork, you dive in like you've been starved for 40 days and 40 nights. Nuggets flying, fries clutched like treasure, sauce dripping down your chin. Smooth, right? Wrong.

The Animal Planet Problem
Eating with your hands when cutlery is available doesn't make you "chill." It makes you look like you've escaped from a wildlife documentary.

Sauce Is Not Cologne
Ketchup on your shirt sleeve isn't "quirky." BBQ sauce on your chin isn't "cute." Condiments belong on the food, not your

face.

The Speed-Eating Disaster

Hoovering down your meal like it's an Olympic sport doesn't impress anyone. It just makes her wonder if you even tasted it or if you might accidentally inhale the fork next.

Pro-Tips for Dining Like a Human

- Utensils Exist for a Reason: Fork. Knife. Spoon. Use them.
- Napkin > Sleeve: Wiping your mouth on your hoodie isn't resourceful, it's gross.
- Chew, Don't Shovel: Slow down. You're not in a race.
- Bonus Move: Offer her fries before you eat all of them. Sharing food = instant brownie points.

Why It Matters

Nobody's expecting five-star table manners. But basic eating skills show self-respect and respect for the person sitting across from you.

So gentlemen, remember you're not a raccoon in a McDonald's bin. Eat like a human being.

Chapter Thirteen: Hair Today, Gone Tomorrow

Your hair is the crown you never take off. But some of you are wearing that crown like it's been dragged through a fryer.

The Oil Slick Situation
Not washing your hair doesn't make it "natural." It makes it shiny in all the wrong ways. If people can see their reflection in your scalp, it's time for shampoo.

Gel Is Not Cement
There's a fine line between "styled" and "helmet." If your hair doesn't move in a hurricane, you're not stylish you're a crash-test dummy.

The Mullet Myth

Yes, mullets came back. No, that doesn't mean you should try it. There are comebacks, and then there are crimes against follicles. Know the difference.

Pro-Tips from the Hair Chair

- Wash Regularly: Shampoo + conditioner = baseline human.
- Trim the Bush: Regular haircuts stop you from drifting into caveman territory.
- Experiment with Care: Bold styles are fine but know the difference between "statement" and "accident."
- Bonus Move: Ask a barber what suits your face. Professionals exist for a reason.

Why It Matters

Your hair is often the first thing people notice. If it's greasy, over-gelled, or mulleted beyond redemption, that's what they'll remember.

So, gentlemen, treat your hair like an asset, not an afterthought. Otherwise, "Hair Today, Gone Tomorrow" might be more of a prophecy than a chapter title.

Chapter Fourteen: Manners Make the Man

Here's the deal: being polite isn't old-fashioned, it's a cheat code. Good manners don't make you weak. They make you stand out in a sea of grunting, hoodie-wiping chaos gremlins.

Please & Thank You: The Power Duo
Two tiny words, massive impact. Saying "please" shows respect. Saying "thank you" shows gratitude. Forget them, and you look like a spoiled brat demanding nuggets from the universe.

Table Manners 101
Chewing with your mouth open? Gross. Talking while food sprays everywhere?

Grosser. Eating like the Cookie Monster? Congratulations you've just guaranteed she's never going out with you again.

Respect Beyond the Table
Holding doors, saying hello, letting someone go first these aren't big gestures, but they signal that you actually care about other humans existing. Shocking, right?

Pro-Tips for Gentleman Mode

- Mind the Volume: Shouting in public doesn't make you cool, it makes you annoying.
- Respect Service Staff: How you treat waiters, cashiers, and delivery drivers says more about you than how you treat your crush.

- Compliments > Insults: Teasing has limits. Don't hide behind "jokes" that are just rude.

- Bonus Move: Saying "thank you" to her parents? That's god-tier boyfriend energy.

Why It Matters

Looks fade. Memes die. Trends vanish. But people always remember how you made them feel. Good manners cost nothing, but they pay off forever.

So gentlemen, remember swagger might get attention, but manners seal the deal.

Chapter Fifteen: Chill, Romeo

So, you've got a crush. Your heart is pounding. Your brain is screaming, "She's the one!" And suddenly you're writing love poems, planning your wedding playlist, and practicing your "Mr. and Mrs." signatures... all before the second date.

Slow down, Shakespeare.

The Overload Effect
Coming on too strong doesn't make you look romantic. It makes you look like a runaway train. Big, dramatic declarations on day two don't scream love they scream clingy and terrifying.

Fantasy vs Reality

Yes, it feels magical when you like someone. But here's the thing: she doesn't know you yet. You can't fast-forward to the grand finale when the intro hasn't even played.

The Balance Move

There's a sweet spot between "shows no interest" and "buys matching grave plots." Find it. Respect the slow build. Relationships aren't speedruns.

Pro-Tips for Pacing Romance

- Take It Slow: First, be friends. Then level up. Don't skip the tutorial.
- Save the Poetry: Write her a poem after a few months, not after exchanging Snapchats.

- Don't Overshare: Pouring your soul out on date one feels like emotional spam.
- Bonus Move: Mystery is attractive. Leave room for her to want to know more.

Why It Matters

If you rush, you risk scaring her off before anything even starts. Real romance isn't about speed it's about timing.

So chill, Romeo. Put down the wedding vows. Pick up patience.

Chapter Sixteen: Respect the Respawn

You shot your shot. She said no. End of the world, right? Wrong. It's not "game over" it's just a respawn.

Rejection ≠ Death
Every guy gets rejected. Every. Single. One. The difference between the gentleman and the banshee is how you handle it. The banshee rages. The gentleman shrugs, learns, and moves on.

Don't Throw a Tantrum
Crying, pouting, or blasting "she broke my heart" TikTok's won't help. Neither will insulting her because she wasn't interested. If you go from "you're amazing" to "you're ugly anyway" in five seconds

flat congratulations, you just told on yourself.

The Reputation Game

Girls talk. If you act like a sore loser, word spreads. If you handle rejection with class, that spreads too and suddenly, you look more attractive, not less.

Pro-Tips for the Respawn Kings

- Take the L Gracefully: Say "no worries" and mean it.
- Don't Trash Talk: It doesn't make you look cool; it makes you look bitter.
- Learn and Level Up: Sometimes it's timing, sometimes it's vibes. Either way, it's experience gained.
- Bonus Move: Treat her with respect after rejection that's how you earn "legend"

status.

Why It Matters

Rejection doesn't define you. Your reaction does. Handle it well, and you build character (and street cred). Handle it badly, and you become a walking red flag.

So gentlemen, respect the respawn. Respawn with dignity, and you'll be ready for the next level.

Chapter Seventeen: Smell Like a Human, Not a Locker Room

You walk into a room. Heads turn. Not because of your charm but because you smell like a forgotten gym bag.
Gentlemen, this is not the legacy you want.

The Sweat Situation
Everyone sweats. It's normal. What's not normal is pretending deodorant is optional. If your armpits could be weaponized, it's time for action.

Cologne Catastrophe
On the flip side: drowning yourself in body spray doesn't solve the problem. It just layers "cheap chemical storm" on top of

"sweat swamp." If people can smell you before they see you, you've overdone it.

Laundry Matters Too

Clean skin + dirty clothes = still gross. That hoodie that's been "airing out" on the chair for a week? Yeah, it's not fresh. Wash it.

Pro-Tips for Smelling Like a Gentleman

- Daily Deodorant: This is non-negotiable. Spray or roll just do it.
- Light Cologne, not a Fog Machine: One or two sprays. Not a fumigation event.
- Wash Your Clothes: Sweat sticks to fabric. Fresh laundry = fresh start.
- Bonus Move: Subtle scent + cleanliness = the combo that actually makes people lean in, not back away.

Why It Matters

Smelling good isn't about being fancy. It's about showing basic respect for the people forced to share air with you.

So, gentlemen, remember aim for "pleasantly human," not "locker room biohazard."

Chapter Eighteen: Sports Talk Isn't Small Talk

You love sports. Great. But here's the cold truth: not everyone wants a 20-minute TED Talk about last night's game. If her eyes glaze over faster than a donut, you've lost her.

Stats ≠ Flirting
Telling a girl how many goals your team scored is not the same as telling her something about you. She's not your coach she doesn't need the play-by-play.

Reading the Room
If she's nodding politely while scrolling her phone, that's not interest. That's survival mode. Learn the signs before you trap

someone in a conversation that feels like overtime with no end.

Balance the Field

Talking about sports is fine if she's into it. But balance it out. Ask her about her interests too. Relationships are a two-way game, not a never-ending commentary.

Pro-Tips for Not Boring Her to Tears

- Test the Waters: Drop a quick sports reference. If she bites, go deeper. If not, switch topics.
- Keep It Short: Headlines, not essays.
- Find Common Ground: If she doesn't like footy, maybe she likes music, movies, or literally anything else.
- Bonus Move: Learn her favorite thing and show interest. That's the real MVP move.

Why It Matters

Sports talk isn't evil. But if it's all you've got, it makes you look one-dimensional. You want her to see you, not just your team colors.

So, gentlemen, remember small talk is about connecting not commentating.

Chapter Nineteen: The Group Chat Isn't Private

You think the group chat is safe. You think the wild memes, trash talk, and embarrassing confessions will stay between the boys. Spoiler: it won't. Screenshots are forever.

The Leak Is Inevitable
All it takes is one "trusted mate" to share a screenshot, and suddenly your inside joke is school-wide gossip. Don't type anything you wouldn't want projected on the big screen at assembly.

Trash Talk Turns Toxic
Roasting each other is fine. But when you start trashing girls, teachers, or anyone

else? Those screenshots become evidence. And guess what? Girls talk too. If they see you're a keyboard warrior in private, you're done.

Jokes Don't Always Land
What's "funny" with the boys can look cruel, creepy, or just plain gross out of context. Screenshots don't capture your tone only your words. And those words last.

Pro-Tips for Surviving Group Chat Drama

- Assume Screenshots Exist: Because they do. Always.
- Think Before You Type: If it would ruin your reputation, don't send it.
- Keep the Roast Clean: Tease your mates, but don't cross into bully territory.
- Bonus Move: Being the guy who doesn't

post cringe is underrated.

Why It Matters

Your reputation isn't just built in public it's built in private too. One dumb screenshot can undo everything.

So, gentlemen, remember: the group chat isn't Vegas. What happens there doesn't stay there.

Chapter Twenty: The Secret Cheat Code

You've showered. You've tamed the socks. You're not roaring like a banshee or eating nuggets like a raccoon. Good start. But here's the ultimate cheat code the move that makes all the difference: listening.

Listening > Talking

Most guys think the way to impress a girl is to talk more, brag more, flex more. Wrong. The real move is shutting up and actually hearing what she's saying.

Why It Works

When you listen, you're telling her: "What you say matters." That's rarer than you think. And trust me, it's way more attractive than your Fortnite kill streak.

It's Not Just Nodding

Listening isn't sitting there saying "yeah, cool" while daydreaming about snacks. It's asking follow-up questions. Showing interest. Actually, remembering what she said last week.

Pro-Tips for Unlocking Gentleman Mode

- Phone Down: Nothing says "I don't care" like scrolling mid-convo.
- Mirror Mode: Reflect back what she said in your own words shows you're paying attention.
- Memory = Magic: Mention something she told you before. Instant bonus points.
- Bonus Move: Listen more than you talk. It feels weird at first. Then it feels powerful.

Why It Matters

Looks fade. Muscles shrink. Memes get old. But people always remember how you made them feel. Listening is how you stand out in a world full of noise.

So, gentlemen, remember: the secret cheat code isn't bigger muscles or smoother lines. It's something much rarer respect. And it starts with listening.

About the Author

Holly Symons has mastered the fine art of saying what everyone else is thinking, but funnier. A writer, creative whirlwind, and lifelong observer of teenage chaos, she has turned her sharp wit into a guidebook for the next generation of gentlemen-in-training.

When she's not roasting bad hygiene, sock crimes, or questionable flirting tactics, Holly writes fantasy adventures, lifestyle books, and the kind of humor that makes even the most stubborn teen boys laugh (while secretly taking notes).

Her mission? To help young men step up their game not with fake bravado, but with respect, self-awareness, and just enough sarcasm to keep it entertaining.

www.ingramcontent.com/pod-product-compliance
Lightning Source LLC
Chambersburg PA
CBHW071222070526
44584CB00019B/3113